ESTA...

IS YOUR
ESTATE PLAN
READY?

As an exclusive and special gift for readers of *It's Not Too Late: How to Protect Your Home and Life Savings in Iowa*, my team and I have created this essential checklist that you can use to assess whether your estate plan will accomplish your wishes.

By answering the questions in *Is Your Estate Plan Ready?* you'll discover whether your will or trust is adequate for your needs and where you might need to shore things up.

Think your will is good enough for you? Take this **EXCLUSIVE ASSESSMENT** and find out for sure!

SPECIAL BONUS GIFT

www.ItsNotTooLateBooks.com/assessment

We learned a lot during our visit with Ethan; and he was unbelievably thorough, patient with all our questions, and never pressured us into any decisions. We had talked about doing our will, but always put it off because we thought we were too young. Best decision we ever made with Ethan!

-- Chad S., Client

Ethan was a great comfort to me during my time of need.

-- Marlys U., Client

The Huizenga Law team has been very helpful in walking through this process with us. We are very lucky to have found them.

-- David B., Client

Ethan did a fantastic job. I was very thankful we got a referral to him.

-- Stacie E., Client

ALSO BY ETHAN HUIZENGA

It's Not Too Late: The Ultimate Guide to Nursing Home Medicaid for the Stressed-Out Husband or Wife

DISCLAIMER

This book is not intended to be legal advice and reading this book does not create an attorney-client relationship between you and the author. Each reader of this book will have unique personal, family, and financial considerations which must be taken into account before any legal advice can be provided. If you are looking for advice about your specific circumstances, you should contact the author directly at 712-737-3885 or by visiting www.huizengalaw.com/book-a-call.

IT'S

How to Protect Your

NOT

Home and Life Savings

TOO

in Iowa

LATE

Volume 2

ETHAN HUIZENGA

Cover Design: Mirko Pohle

Published by: **It's Not Too Late Books, L.L.C.**

Paperback ISBN: 979-8-9850496-1-9

Printed in the United States of America.

118 Second Street NW
Orange City, IA 51041

Ph: (712) 737-3885
www.itsnottoolatebooks.com

CONTENTS

WHO SHOULD READ THIS BOOK?

You've heard the horror stories:

- When Grandpa remarried after Grandma died, his new wife and her kids ended up with half the family farm and all his money.
- I can't leave anything to my daughter. If her husband gets his hands on one dollar, he'll turn around and spend five.
- Uncle Jerry spent hundreds of thousands of dollars on the nursing home. Now there's no money left, and his kids have to sell his house.
- My neighbor died and now his kids refuse to speak to each other.

And of course, there's that "four-letter word": <u>probate</u>.

Whether you've seen the badness up close or read about family fallout in the news or on social media, the fact is every horror story out there is an example of a threat that went unnoticed or unaddressed.

This book is for the person who doesn't want to be another horror story.

You see, while many of the estate planning decisions you can make boil down to what happens with your money, the motivations behind those decisions are almost never, ultimately, about money.

I wrote this book for the person who doesn't want their personal finances to be supervised by a judge. It's for the person who doesn't want their mental and physical health to become a matter public record.

If you have a parent or grandparent who sold their house and spent every penny of their life savings at the nursing home, but you don't want that to happen to you, then you need to read this book.

You should read this book if you want your spouse to live comfortably when you're gone, but you want to guarantee your assets end up with your kids even if your spouse remarries.

If you want to leave a safety net for your children – one that can't be taken away by a creditor, a lawsuit, or that no-good son-in-law, I wrote this book for you.

But most of all, I wrote this book for the person who wants to preserve what resources they can, so they can leave their loved ones with a meaningful personal and financial legacy.

Legacy is a small word with a big impact. "Legacy is about learning from the past, living in the present, and building for the future" (legacyproject.org).

Your legacy is made up of the collection of lessons you've learned, the faith and philosophy that you follow, and the resources you've built during your life. But it doesn't become a legacy until you pass it on to the people who are important to you.

You've built your legacy in anticipation of handing it over to your loved ones. At its root, that's a lot like hope. Hope is an optimism that the future will work out in your favor.

This book is for the person who believes that hope, without a plan, is just a dream.

Turn the page and read on if you're ready to stop dreaming and start planning.

"A goal without a plan is just a wish."

Antoine de Saint-Exupéry

MY PROMISE TO YOU

I've been helping people with their estate planning for long enough to figure out at least one thing: the last thing anyone wants to do is take time out of their busy life to think about their death.

And going to the lawyer's office to do it might be the only thing worse than going to the dentist (no offense to dentists).

Yet, just like a toothache, what happens at the end of our lives is both the last thing anyone wants to think about and the thing that keeps people up at night.

I recently met with a husband and wife who were losing sleep over what to do for their disabled son. Over the last year he has spent weeks at a time in the hospital due to a chronic illness. His disability makes it difficult for him to work. They were desperate to set things up so he would be taken care of when they are gone.

Did I mention they don't trust his wife?

The first lawyer they talked to was too busy to help them find a solution. The second lawyer they met with actually told them to cut their son out completely! They wanted a better result.

Using the tools described in Chapters 3-6 and the process outlined in Chapter 7, this couple designed a plan that would provide for all of their kids equally, ensure the family farm passed to their grandchildren, and protect the inheritance from creditors, predators, and in-laws.

They got peace of mind and hope for their family's financial future.

That's leaving a legacy.

Whether you're concerned about family dynamics or the in-laws, health issues for yourself or your loved ones, or passing down a family farm or business, you deserve the peace of mind that comes from having a plan in place.

Not just any plan, either. You deserve a plan that serves your specific needs, your unique circumstances. And you shouldn't have to dread going to the lawyer's office to "get your will done."

So, here's my commitment to you: if you will take a couple of hours out of your schedule to read this book, I promise you will learn: 1) why having no plan at all will be more painful than doing the planning, 2) the tools you can use to leave a legacy that is meaningful for you and your kids, and

3) a foolproof process you can follow to make the whole experience as painless as possible.

Along the way, I'm going to share specific estate planning strategies to solve the four major threats to your legacy: incapacity, probate, creditors and predators, and nursing home costs.

On top of all that, you'll hear real life stories from my clients (with the details changed – no confidentiality breaches here), people just like you who followed the process in this book to design a plan that fit their family and found peace of mind in the process.

This book won't give you all the answers for your situation. That's impossible without meeting together to discuss your goals and concerns.

But I am going to show you the path to a plan that preserves your legacy. If you want more specific answers for your specific situation, I encourage you to schedule a free 15-minute Exploration Call with me at www.huizengalaw.com/book-a-call.

"Hope is not a course of action."

Vince Lombardi

WHAT IS ESTATE PLANNING?

Everybody knows the answer to that, right? Estate planning is when you go down to the lawyer and get your will done.

You may have guessed already: that's not a very good definition of estate planning. After all, if that's all there is to it, I wouldn't have written a 100-page book about it!

In my law firm, we're redefining estate planning in Northwest Iowa. I would humbly submit the following as a better definition of estate planning:

Estate planning means ensuring you are in control of yourself and your finances while you're alive and well. It means taking care of yourself and your loved ones when you become incapacitated. And it means giving what you have to the people you want, when you want, in the way you want.

There's a lot in there to unpack, so let's look at each part separately.

CONTROL WHILE YOU'RE ALIVE AND WELL

This one seems like a no-brainer, right? It's your body, your physical care, your money, and your stuff. You should be in charge for as long as possible.

Unfortunately, many people don't consider this when they make decisions.

For example, one common mistake people make is adding one or more of their kids to their bank account. Why would this create a problem? It takes control of your funds out of your hands.

A person with the ability to write and sign checks or, worse yet, a person listed as a co-owner of your account can do anything they want with the money in that account. The bank can't stop them, which means you won't discover a problem until after a withdrawal occurs.

It's out of your control!

But control is a bigger issue than just the people who have access to your bank accounts.

Capacity is the word lawyers use to describe a person's ability to understand a decision or perform an act, and it's at the heart of every question about control.

If your doctor asks you to make a decision about treatment or surgery, you have the capacity to answer the question if you can both understand the benefits, risks, and alternatives and communicate your wishes.

To put it another way, control over your medical care and living arrangements requires that you be able to give **informed consent**.

But the capacity question is different when it comes to financial or "business" decisions. Control over your finances and financial transactions depends on what type of decision is involved.

Testamentary capacity is the most basic level of capacity, so we'll start there. Testamentary capacity is involved in any decisions you make regarding your last will and testament. A person has testamentary capacity if they know who their family is and which stuff is their stuff. Testamentary capacity is personal to you and, generally speaking, your ability to make a will can't be delegated to someone else.

Donative capacity is the next level up and applies to giving gifts during your life. Donative capacity and testamentary capacity are very similar: in both cases, you have to know what you have and who you're giving it to.

But donative capacity also requires that the gift-giver understand the nature, purpose, and effect of the gift as well as the nature and extent of the property being given. Since the gift happens right away (as opposed to after your death), <u>you need to know how much control you're giving up</u> by making that gift.

Unlike with testamentary capacity, it is possible to give someone else the authority to give gifts on your behalf.

The final level of control falls under **contractual capacity**. Contractual capacity describes your ability to understand the nature of any agreement you are making. This level of capacity is unique to each separate transaction. Your ability to sell your car requires a different level of understanding than your ability to sign a mortgage.

As long as you're alive and well, you get to make decisions about your physical needs and your financial affairs. But what happens if your capacity diminishes as you age?

TAKING CARE OF YOURSELF AND YOUR LOVED ONES AFTER YOUR INCAPACITY

We know capacity is your ability to understand a decision or perform an act. But when you lose that ability, you need someone else to step in to take care of your affairs.

That's the second part of our definition of estate planning: setting up instructions ahead of time, so you can have confidence that your plan for your physical care and your financial resources continues even when someone else is involved.

In order to keep your wishes as the driving force behind the decision-making, you'll want to give instructions about how your family and advisors will know whether you are incapacitated, who takes over in that situation, and what things they can or should have authority over.

Depending on your goals, you can give the substitute decisionmaker discretion over how to make decisions or you can give specific instructions that they have to follow. (In most cases, you'll want to use a blend of these two approaches.)

> Simply adding your children to your bank account takes control of the account out of your hands.

If that's how you can take care of <u>yourself</u> if you become incapacitated, what can you do to take care of your loved ones in that situation?

There are two main areas that we think about in this regard: 1) access to resources and 2) conflict avoidance.

The most common approach my clients use to take care of their loved ones is to prevent conflict through clear communication ahead of time.

Your incapacity will probably be a stressful or even traumatic time of transition for your loved ones. If you plan ahead <u>and communicate the details of that plan</u>, you will help your loved ones navigate the transition with grace.

But it can be just as important to make sure your spouse and dependents have access to your financial resources to help with their day-to-day expenses. The problem is that the law presumes that a person's financial resources should be used for their own support.

Spending your money on someone else is, by the law's definition, not in your best interests. So, if you want your spouse or your children to have access to your bank accounts, retirement accounts, or property if you become incapacitated, you'll need to give instructions granting them that access.

There are a few different tools you can use to implement your incapacity plan, including financial and medical power of attorney documents (more on these in Chapter 6) and two different types of trusts (see Chapter 5).

"Wait. Hold on," you may be thinking. "I thought you used a trust to avoid probate when you die." And you'd be right, but maybe not in the way you expect (we'll get into more detail on that in the Chapter 4).

If you define *probate* as "the court case your family suffers through after your death," then you're correct that trusts also help transition your stuff from you to your loved ones.

And if "getting your will done" is the same as "deciding who gets your stuff and when," then this last part of our definition is what most people think of as estate planning.

WHO, HOW, AND WHEN: GIVING WHAT YOU HAVE TO YOUR LOVED ONES ON YOUR TERMS

You know who you want to give your money, home, and heirlooms to. But have you thought about how or when that change will happen?

Let me tell you about a client of mine, we'll call her "Mary."

EXAMPLE

Mary was worried that she was going to be forced to sell the house where she had lived for 56 years (51 of those with her late husband) to pay her future nursing home bill. She read online that if you wait five years to apply for Medicaid you can give your assets away. So, Mary gifted her house to her daughter.

A year later, Mary's daughter lost her job. With no money coming in to pay the bills, she decided Mary would have to pay rent in order to stay in her own home! Since Mary had given her daughter full ownership of the house, she had two options: pay rent or be evicted.

Another year later, Mary's daughter and son-in-law went through a messy divorce due to the stress of their financial difficulties. Since Mary's rent payments helped pay expenses like her daughter's house payment, utilities, and groceries, Mary's house got tangled up in the divorce proceedings and very nearly went to her (ex) son-in-law instead of her daughter.

Yikes.

Mary started out fine. She just wanted to protect her house from the nursing home bill. But everything went off the rails after that. She didn't consider what it would mean if someone else owned the home she lived in. Giving the house to her daughter ultimately meant Mary's needs didn't or couldn't take priority.

She knew who should get her house and she knew when that needed to happen. But she didn't think about how and went about it the wrong way.

Imagine what would have happened if her daughter was forced to file for bankruptcy. At best, Mary might have had to buy her home back from her daughter!

Or what if her daughter had died? Mary would have been at the mercy of her daughter's own estate planning. Not good.

In the end, this story worked out. Mary moved out of her home and into an assisted living facility, allowing her daughter to sell the house and use the proceeds to buy her own home after the divorce.

But only after some sleepless nights and frantic planning sessions with our office!

With thoughtful planning about how to get her house to her daughter, Mary could have protected her home from the nursing home during her lifetime without risking loss of that home in her daughter's divorce or to her daughter's creditors.

That's what we did for "Susan." Susan had some money in savings, but her primary asset was the family farm where she lived. Using one of the trusts discussed in Chapter 5, we helped Susan protect the farm while she was living and pass it to her sole child when she died.

Better yet, we set up creditor and divorce protection for Susan's daughter which gave Susan the peace of mind that the family farm would stay in the family for her grandchildren as well.

Mary's story illustrates what can happen when planning isn't done properly. But what happens when planning isn't done at all? The government has the answer, and we'll explore that in the next chapter.

> "By failing to prepare,
> you are preparing to fail."
>
> Ben Franklin

CHAPTER I

THE GOVERNMENT HAS A PLAN FOR YOU

That sounds very dystopian, doesn't it? And it should! What business does the government have telling you how to manage your finances or how to take care of your health and physical needs?

But that's exactly what will happen if you opt out of creating your own estate plan.

Don't worry. The government's plan isn't all "Skynet" and black ops. You'll simply have no say over who makes medical decisions for you. You'll have to spend your savings to pay for long-term care when you need it. And your personal affairs will become public record through court cases both during and after your life.

Okay. You should definitely worry about the government's plan.

THE GOVERNMENT ISN'T THERE FOR YOUR FAMILY

You already know what dealing with the government is like. You file your taxes, follow the speed limit, and shovel your snow within 10 hours of accumulation. There are countless ways the government is involved in our everyday lives.

Unfortunately, if you don't make your own estate plan, the government will also intervene in decisions about your physical care and your finances after you become incapacitated.

We lovingly call that process "living probate." The legal terms are **guardianship** and **conservatorship**.

When you don't appoint someone to serve as your agent for medical decisions, the government creates an order of priority for those decisions. It goes like this, generally:

1. Your spouse
2. Your children
3. Your parents

Which is all well and good in theory, but how does that go in practice? What happens when your children disagree with your spouse or, if you aren't married, what if your children disagree with each other? What if your family's beliefs about medical care and treatment are drastically different from yours?

Worse yet: what if no one in your family is willing to step up?

The only other option is to open a guardianship. A **guardianship** is a court case where someone – called your guardian – is appointed by a judge to make decisions about your physical care.

In a guardianship, the guardian has to establish that you don't have the capacity to act in your own best interests regarding your safety or your basic daily needs. They file an initial report documenting your physical and mental condition as well as a care plan, both of which require approval from a judge.

If no one in your family is willing to take on the responsibility of being your medical decisionmaker, guardianship gets even more complicated. For example, a close friend probably can't ask to be appointed to care for you under the guardianship statutes. Of course, if all else fails, the state of Iowa has a government office that can step in as your guardian if necessary.

If a guardianship involves "care of the person," then a **conservatorship** is the court-supervised "care of the finances." Just like with a guardianship, the conservator has to prove that a substitute decisionmaker is necessary because you can't make good decisions regarding your financial affairs.

> You should definitely worry about
> the government's plan.

In both the of these court cases, you will have an attorney appointed to represent you. The guardian and/or conservator will have their own attorney. And your family may also have their own attorney. That's two, maybe three, lawyer bills on top of the court costs.

If there is a disagreement over what the best approach is, the court will hold hearings where your family's "dirty laundry" gets aired out in public.

In order to get appointed, the guardian will have to provide documentation of your physical or mental condition, and the conservator will have to provide a description of your financial situation. Then, any time a major decision needs to be made, they will have to get permission from the court.

Even if nothing changes in a given year, a guardian or conservator must file annual reports, giving the court regular updates on your medical and financial status.

Between the initial costs to set up the case and the ongoing reporting requirements, living probate can cost your family thousands.

Oh - did I mention that court cases are matters of public record? That means all of this happens in a way that gives anyone and everyone front row seats to your personal affairs.

EXAMPLE

A few years ago, I had an elderly client, Lucy, who went through some difficult life events – her husband and her son died within days of each other. Her mental and physical health spiraled downward as she mourned until one day her neighbor called an ambulance because Lucy was wandering around her front yard without a coat in the middle of an Iowa February.

IT'S NOT TOO LATE

I first met with Lucy's family because, after her frostbite healed, the hospital told them Lucy couldn't go back to her own house. She needed supervision to keep her safe, so they wanted to admit her to an assisted living facility. The problem was, Lucy hadn't appointed anyone to make decisions on her behalf.

Sitting in my conference room, all four kids verbally agreed that the oldest daughter should be appointed as guardian and conservator. It's what happened when they weren't all sitting in my conference room together that made this story so sad.

Less than a week after that meeting, Lucy's four remaining children had divided into two sides, boys versus girls. After several months and a long hearing, we were finally able to get the oldest daughter appointed as guardian and conservator, but the brothers harassed her so much that she stopped taking their calls and, ultimately, resigned.

The family conflict and the stress of being a court-appointed decisionmaker caused her health to suffer. Her brothers made it so she couldn't focus on being a daughter to Lucy.

In the end, Lucy's youngest son took Lucy to a different lawyer who prepared a deed to transfer her house to him. After that, Lucy's daughters finally just closed the court case, and the youngest son took over the decision-making.

Lucy still lives in the assisted living facility, but I don't think the sisters and brothers are on speaking terms to this day.

Fortunately, you can avoid the government's plan by making one of your own. But if you don't, your family members may be pitted against each other in a public court case.

I don't know about you, but I don't want my loved ones to go through that trying to take care of me.

THE GOVERNMENT ISN'T THERE FOR YOU

Not only does the government's plan stand in the way of your family taking care of you, it also interferes with your ability to leave a financial legacy the way you want.

Let's start with nursing home costs. The government makes funds available to pay your nursing home bills while you're living through the Medicaid system. But if you want to access those funds, you must navigate a complicated system of confusing conditions and strict financial requirements.

If you make one misstep, you're stuck consuming your life savings at the rate of $8,000 per month – or more – to pay the nursing home bill. Say goodbye to that financial legacy you worked so hard to build!

Once again, you can avoid this problem if you make your own plan ahead of time. We'll talk about what you can do now, before the nursing home gets involved, in Chapter 5.

> If your spouse is already in a nursing home, there's a different solution. Check out my book *It's Not Too Late: The Ultimate Guide to Nursing Home Medicaid for the Stressed Out Husband or Wife* to learn how you can keep your home and life savings while your spouse gets help from Medicaid (Title 19).

Second, the government also has a set of instructions to help distribute your life savings after your death. If you don't take the time to plan your final affairs now, the laws of **intestate succession** determine who gets your money and property.

It's as complicated and frustrating as it sounds.

Just this week I met with a husband and wife who had some very specific concerns about how their assets would be allocated to their children. The wife told me a terribly sad story about her dad's estate.

EXAMPLE

After a long period of mourning following his first wife's death from cancer, John met and married Jill, and they moved into John's home where they lived for 15 years.

While John and Jill were famously happy together, John's kids and Jill's kids never quite saw eye to eye.

> Just a few years ago, John passed away after a major stroke. John didn't have a will in place, but he did have his residence and a couple of joint accounts with Jill.
>
> Unbeknownst to John's kids, John had put the house into his and Jill's names a few years before his death. With everything held in joint tenancy, Iowa law gave all of John's assets to Jill automatically. When Jill passed away a few months later, her will left everything to her kids.
>
> John's kids inherited nothing from their dad.

Because of the wife's personal experiences, this couple was adamant that they would do whatever it took to ensure no one but their kids would get their hard-earned money or the home they had built together. Her dad never wanted to talk about it because he assumed it would all work out the way he wanted. Instead, the government's plan left it all to his step-kids in the end.

Finally, even if you take the step of putting together a will that explains your wishes, the government will intervene in your affairs to supervise the process of passing your assets to your loved ones. This oversight is called **probate**.

A few pages back, we talked about the horrors of "living probate." After your death, we're talking about plain, old, run-of-the-mill **probate**. You've probably heard of it. Probate is the "four-letter word" of estate planning. It's in the urban legend category. As in, "Everybody knows you don't want to go through probate."

But what is probate exactly?

Probate is the government-created, court-supervised process of transitioning your home and life savings to your loved ones. It happens in court, which means court costs. It requires a lawyer, which means lawyer fees. And it was designed by the government, so it comes with all the efficiency of any bureaucracy.

Picture the DMV, but less fun.

As a court case, probate is a public proceeding, so all the details of your financial life and your family's...we'll call them quirks...are on display in a public forum. Anyone who wants to know your net worth or wants to see how much money your daughter inherited can look it up with a few taps on the iPad screen.

Everyone gets to watch when your youngest son throws a tantrum because your oldest daughter got the Velvet Elvis or the singing Billy the Bigmouth Bass.

The only reason it's better than parenting a toddler is because you're not there to be embarrassed by it.

Maybe you're thinking, "My kids won't fight like that over my stuff. They get along so great!" You're probably right; most families don't split when a parent passes away. But I'd hazard a guess that you don't want the whole world looking in on your finances or seeing what you've left behind for your kids.

And don't forget: everybody gets along great right up until the moment they don't. The strain of losing mom or dad combined with a frustrating, bureaucratic process that doesn't always make sense can bring out the worst in anyone.

As you may have guessed, there are other options besides the government's plan. Check out the next chapter to learn the most common tool people start with – and why that might not be the best option.

"Planning is bringing the future into the present so you can do something about it now."

Alan Lakein

CHAPTER 2

WHERE THERE'S A WILL, THERE'S A PLAN

We're going to start with the elephant in the room: getting your will in place.

The term *will* is short for "last will and testament." Your will is your final (last) statement (testament) of your wishes (will). As the final statement of your wishes, a will is, by definition, completely useless during your life.

Put another way, your will only takes effect after your death. Your executor has no power to act until after you pass away. Your will won't pass your property on to your loved ones until your death.

In fact, your will doesn't do anything to protect your assets, not from long-term care costs while you're living and not from your or your kids' creditors after your death.

A will is a unique legal document. For it to be valid, it must be signed by you and two witnesses, and each of the signers needs to be present when the other two people sign. Then, since it represents your express instructions, we have to take your will into court to make sure your wishes are

13

followed completely and accurately. That's the probate process we talked about in the last chapter.

To get probate started, the person you chose to be in charge submits your will to a judge along with statements from the witnesses who watched you sign it. The judge must confirm that the will is valid before the person in charge can do anything else.

Once probate has started, your financial status becomes public record through various court filings, and the whole world can see the inheritance you left for your loved ones.

But you still need a will if you want to avoid the government's plan for dividing up your home and life savings. That's because your will does three main things for you:

1. It directs who will get your property when you die;
2. It designates your executor; and
3. It names a guardian for your minor children.

Let's explore each of these functions separately.

WHO GETS YOUR STUFF?

The most well-known reason to set up your will is defining who gets your property when you die. Generally speaking, these instructions apply to all the assets you own individually: your house, car, bank accounts, clothing, furniture, heirlooms, collections, investments, and so forth.

When you identify who will receive your "stuff" after your death, those people or organizations become your **beneficiaries**. There is no limit on who you can include as a beneficiary in your will.

Your wishes can be as broad as, "Give everything to my spouse." You can leave percentages to your favorite charities. You can impose conditions on when and how your kids will receive their share of your money.

Because your will doesn't take effect until your death, all of these instructions can be changed right up until you pass away (as long as you have capacity, that is).

WHO GETS CONROL?

I've mentioned a few times already that estate planning is about keeping you in control while you're alive and well. Part of that control involves choosing who will manage and distribute your assets when you are gone. You designate that person or company in your will.

Since your will dictates who will inherit the assets you own in just your name, someone needs to oversee that process. There are lots of titles for that person, but Iowa dubs them the **executor** or the **personal representative**.

A description and explanation of the role of executor could really fill its own book, so I'm just going to give you a couple of important highlights here.

First, the executor is responsible for winding up your final affairs. This includes paying any income taxes or debts you owe, collecting on any debts other people owe you, taking care of and protecting your property until distribution, and following the directions provided in your will.

Second, the executor is a fiduciary which means they are required to act only according to the best interests of the beneficiaries under your will. Often, this means balancing your kids' competing desires and expectations.

Finally, while your executor is named by you in the will, they are officially appointed by a court. This means they won't have access to your financial information until they submit your will to probate (we talked about that process in the last chapter). It also means they are subject to the supervision of a judge and can be called into court if they aren't doing their job adequately.

With all those obligations and duties, the choice of executor is pretty important. In fact, one of the most common questions I get from clients is, "Who should I appoint as my executor?" Unfortunately, that's a really difficult question to answer since everyone has different needs, expectations, and relationships.

Some things to consider as you decide who will be your executor include a person's knowledge or expertise, their geographic location, and their relationship with your beneficiaries. Maybe the most overlooked approach to choosing your executor is to just ask your loved ones for their input. It never hurts to ask!

In the sense that an executor is a role that is specific and unique to a will, you can't appoint an executor without having a will. But there are other ways to appoint a person to distribute your assets at your death (we'll talk more about that in Chapter 4 and Chapter 5).

However, in Iowa there is one position that you have to fill using your last will and testament no matter what approach you use for dividing your assets: the guardian for your kids.

> If you're trying to decide on the right person for a role in your estate plan, I've put together some short guides to help you weigh all the important factors. You can download them from my reader-only resource webpage by visiting www.itsnottoolatebooks.com/resources.

WHO GETS THE KIDS?

If one main point of an estate plan is to protect your estate for the benefit of the people you leave behind, then the most important thing you can hope to protect with your estate plan is your children.

This last aspect of writing your will is crucially important for the parents of children who are under age 18. Who will be legally responsible for taking care of your kids if something happens to you and your spouse?

The title for that person is **guardian**. Like the executor, they are appointed by the court based on the terms of your will.

We talked about the role of guardian a bit in Chapter 1 where we described it as "care of the person." While this guardianship is similar in purpose (care of your children), the situation for your minor children is a bit different than the guardianship process for an adult who has no plan.

Unlike the living probate situation, in the case where both you and your spouse have passed away with a well-drafted will, your preference for guardian will have priority over an outside person (including your other family members).

ONE TOOL IN THE TOOLBOX

As we learned in Chapter 1, probate is a key part of the government's plan for your estate. Unfortunately, your will, as important a tool as it is, won't do anything to keep you and your family out of the probate process.

To do that, you'll need several different tools in place. We'll start by looking at some options for keeping assets out of probate at your death in the next chapter.

"Making a plan without the right tools is like making spaghetti without a pot."

Kris Hughes

CHAPTER 3

AVOIDING PROBATE AND NOT MUCH ELSE

Even though your will is a final expression of your wishes regarding your property, it can only direct the distribution of assets in your name and your name only.

Putting it another way, there's a long list of assets your will <u>does not</u> control. These assets fit in a few categories, and you can avoid probate by allocating your assets into one or more of these non-testamentary categories.

CATEGORY ONE: BENEFICIARY DESIGNATIONS

Financial assets – life insurance, annuities, retirement or investment accounts, and even bank accounts – are contractual arrangements with a company who promises a future benefit or holds your funds at your direction.

Within the contract between you and the company is an agreement that the company will pay out the benefit or account balance to people or entities you have designated. This agreement is called a **beneficiary designation**.

Beneficiary designations on your financial assets will keep those assets out of probate because the company doesn't need a court order to distribute the funds to your named beneficiaries. In fact, if they refuse to do so, they can be held responsible for violating the contract governing the account.

Beneficiary designations can be both flexible and frustrating. On the one hand, you can choose any person or entity you want as the beneficiary. On the other hand, if the person or entity you choose doesn't fit with the financial company's preconceptions of who is allowed to receive your assets, they will not let you include that person or entity as a beneficiary.

By default, if you have a financial account that <u>could</u> have a beneficiary designation, but you <u>have not</u> completed the necessary forms to appoint a beneficiary, that account will pass through probate. You can even list your probate estate as the beneficiary of such an account. In either case, your last will and testament determines how that account gets divided.

CATEGORY TWO: CO-OWNERSHIP

Another common method of avoiding probate is to change the ownership of your assets, adding someone else to the title. If you own your house by yourself, your house passes under the terms of your will. But, by adding another person to the title of your house, you can cause the house to pass to that person outside of the probate process. We'll look at two uses of this approach.

One common method of co-ownership is called **joint tenancy with full rights of survivorship,** sometimes just called "joint tenancy." If you own your house with someone else in joint tenancy, your house passes automatically to the other owner(s) and bypasses your will.

Joint tenancy is a common arrangement for married couples on their bank accounts, investment accounts, vehicles, and homes. In these arrangements, the account or property doesn't really change hands when one spouse dies. Instead, it simply stays in the name of the surviving spouse.

While that might be the intention for a married couple, many people make the mistake of listing a child as a joint owner on their checking account. This is a mistake for two reasons.

For one thing, the child who is listed as joint owner becomes an owner. That means they have full control of and access to the money in the account and can do anything they want with it. Putting it another way, it's not illegal for them to take money out of an account they own, so a co-owner can spend the money in the account on themselves.

For another thing, because the account passes to the joint owner automatically when the other owner dies, that child is not required to share the account proceeds with their siblings. The result is often that one child inherits a bigger share of the parent's money than their siblings.

Another way to change ownership of your property involves the use of a **life estate**. A life estate arrangement involves splitting ownership of the property between the present (today) and the future (tomorrow). This approach is most commonly used with real estate.

In a life estate arrangement, there are two owners of the property. The owner of the present interest (today) is called the **life tenant**. The owner of the future interest (tomorrow) is called the **remainderman**. Because the remainderman is already identified as an owner of the property, ownership changes to the future interest holder automatically when you pass away, and the life estate will avoid probate.

Once again, though, there are drawbacks to this arrangement. While the remainderman can't limit the life tenant's reasonable use of the property, the life tenant can't sell or transfer the property without involving the remainderman.

In fact, as a co-owner, the remainderman and the life tenant will split the sale proceeds if the property is sold. Depending on the specifics of the arrangement and the property, this often results in income tax liability for the remainderman.

CATEGORY 3: OUTRIGHT GIFTS

The last way to keep your assets out of probate is to simply give them to the people you want to have them. After all, if it doesn't belong to you, then it's not part of your estate and doesn't go through probate.

But there are big issues with this approach, as one of my clients discovered the hard way.

EXAMPLE

Four years ago, Elinor met with the lawyer in her small town looking for help protecting her home from being sold to pay a nursing home bill if she ever needed long-term care.

After some discussion, the lawyer advised Elinor to deed her house to her daughter, Karen. At that time, Elinor and Susan were on good terms, so she signed the deed taking her name off the title and adding Karen's.

Fast forward to today, and Elinor and Karen not only are not speaking to each other, but Karen has taken legal action to force Elinor to either pay rent or move out of her own home!

Elinor's case is an extreme example, but it's not actually all that uncommon for issues like this to arise after gifting your property to your children.

Remember Mary? (If not, you can check out her story at the end of the Introduction.) Her situation is another example of how giving up control by gifting your assets to your kids with no strings attached can cause problems for you.

And as if that wasn't bad enough, outright gifting can also cost you and your kids money. For example: if you gift your house to your children now and they sell it when you move to a senior living facility or after your death, your kids will be responsible for capital gains taxes on the sale proceeds.

If you had kept it in your name, you would probably have had an exemption from capital gains tax because it was your primary residence.

IT'S NOT JUST ABOUT PROBATE

With so many simple ways to pass your assets to your loved ones at the end of your life, it can be tempting to focus on avoiding probate by using these strategies. But probate's not the only threat to your legacy.

We spent a lot of time in the first couple chapters talking about incapacity and what happens when you can't manage your own affairs anymore. These beneficiary designations, co-ownership arrangements, and outright gifts don't do much to address that problem.

We've also talked about the government's approach to dealing with your home and life savings using the probate process. While each of the three categories described in this chapter do help you avoid the probate process, there are problems with each approach: lack of control during life (co-ownership and gifting), lack of control after death (all three!), and one we haven't talked about—nursing home expenses.

Part of our definition of estate planning included giving what you have to the people you want, when you want, in the way you want. At $7,710 per month (in Iowa as of 2022), one major thing that stands in the way of that is the nursing home bill.

There are four main ways to pay that big monthly expense when a person needs 24-hour care in a facility.

1. Medicare (with lots of conditions and limitations),
2. Long-term care insurance,
3. Spending your life savings, and
4. Government assistance from Medicaid.

There are other sources of funding that are available in the right situation – things like the Veterans Administration's Aid and Attendance benefit or a family member – but for most people, these four sources of funds make up the whole list.

Medicare is the federal health insurance program for seniors and disabled individuals. Its nursing home coverage is minimal, providing coverage only in certain situations and for a relatively short amount of time.

The general rule is that Medicare will cover skilled nursing care for as long as 100 days if the patient was admitted to the hospital for treatment for a total of at least three days prior to moving to the nursing home and only if the patient continues to improve over the course of those 100 days.

Once the patient reaches a "plateau" – meaning their progress levels off – the Medicare coverage stops, even if it's been less than 100 days.

When the Medicare coverage switches off (or if it wasn't available in the first place), the nursing home resident needs to look to the other three sources of funding.

If you have it, long-term care insurance may cover some or all of the bill. For someone fortunate enough to have full, life-time coverage, the insurance company pays out each month and covers the entire cost of the long-term care. More commonly, though, the insurance benefit isn't sufficient to cover all the charges each month and/or it's limited to a term of 1-5 years.

If you don't have long-term care insurance or your insurance doesn't cover the entire expense, then you need to either pay for the nursing home yourself using your life savings or look for outside help, usually from Medicaid.

Without digging too deep into it, Medicaid is a federal-state partnership that, among other things, will pay for the costs of long-term care for people who meet certain strict financial requirements.

For example, the Medicaid rules say that an applicant may not have more than $2,000 of countable assets. If the applicant is married, their spouse can keep half of the total countable assets, but only up to a certain amount. Anything beyond these resource allowances puts the applicant over the limit and makes them ineligible.

Assets that you own are counted toward these resource allowances, so if you add a co-owner, create a life estate, or just identify a beneficiary, those assets will still interfere with your Medicaid eligibility.

Then, even if your countable resources are below the cap and you get Medicaid coverage, the state will come back to your family after your death and require them to liquidate all your assets, whether countable or not, to pay them back. This is called **estate recovery**.

For estate recovery purposes in Iowa, "estate" does not only mean your probate estate. Iowa has expanded the definition of estate to include jointly held assets, trusts you are a beneficiary of, and **retained life estates** (life estates you create yourself). Putting it another way, Iowa estate recovery will collect from any asset you own or have an interest in at the moment just before you take your last breath.

The natural question you might be asking at this point is, "Can I just give my assets to my kids?" Unfortunately, the answer has to be no. You can't give assets away then apply for benefits, and you really can't give assets away once you're on Medicaid.

The rules impose a five-year **lookback** on all gifting. This lookback period begins on the first day of the month when the applicant is found to be otherwise eligible. Then, the state looks back in time for all of the transfers that occurred during the previous 60 months.

All transfers within that five-year period are totaled up to determine the transfer amount. The transfer amount is then divided by a number the state has determined to be the average cost of nursing home care at the time of application. The result is a period of time that the applicant <u>will not receive coverage from Medicaid</u> for their nursing home stay <u>even though they do not have enough money to pay the nursing home bill</u>.

> If you're married and need long-term care ***right now***, all these requirements can seem insurmountable. But it's not too late. Learn about your options in my first book:
>
> *It's Not Too Late: The Ultimate Guide to Nursing Home Medicaid for the Stressed Out Husband or Wife*

ALMOST BUT NOT QUITE

You may have picked up this book because you're looking for a better way to pass your assets to your kids. Probate is a big fear for many people, and (as we've seen) there are lots of ways to avoid probate. But so far we haven't talked about any perfect solutions.

Nursing home expenses are another problem on the horizon. If you have long-term care insurance, the nursing home bill might be covered for awhile. If you don't have insurance, that $7,000-$9,000 monthly expense will consume your life savings pretty quickly. Unless you can get help from a program like Medicaid.

Unfortunately, at this point you probably wouldn't be eligible for help because you own too many countable assets. You want to give some of your money away, but between the possibility of a penalty on your Medicaid application and the issues Mary (p. xvi) and Elinor (p. 25) experienced after giving their assets outright to their kids and giving up control, you're looking for a better approach.

You, like many of my clients, might be asking: "Is there an estate planning tool that can help me avoid probate and protect my savings without giving up control of my assets?"

The answer is yes. And we'll talk about it in the next two chapters.

> "Trust me, I'm a lawyer."
>
> Anonymous

CHAPTER 4

TRUST ME

When I was a law student, the Student Bar Association at the law school – that's like the student government association from college days – sold t-shirts for one of their fundraisers. I didn't buy one, but I remember them clearly.

The front of the shirt said, "Trust me…I'm almost a lawyer."

FIGURE 1

(As an aside, a quick Google search tells me you can still buy these shirts—like the one in Figure 1 from www.teeshirtpalace.com—for your favorite law student.)

If there's one thing I've learned in my almost 15-year career as an elder law and estate planning lawyer, it's that people lean on the people they trust. That's true of the lawyer they hire, but it's even more true about their family.

In the last chapter, we talked a lot about adding kids as owners of your assets. When you make someone else the owner of your home or bank account, you trust that they will take special care of those things. Your hope—maybe even your expectation—is that they won't do anything contrary to your best interests.

Remember Vince Lombardi? According to him, "Hope is not a course of action." From a legal perspective, hope isn't enforceable. It's not binding on the other person.

But, as it turns out, there's a tool in estate planning that documents your hopes and desires in a way that makes them binding and enforceable. Conveniently, this tool is called a **trust**.

As we saw in the last chapter, when you arrange your financial position based on hope instead of documenting your wishes, you put your home and life savings out of your control and expose them to a wide array of risk.

In many cases, the risk is external—someone outside your family goes after your home or life savings or you give up income tax or asset protection advantages. But sometimes (like in Elinor's case on page 25) the family member you trusted with your financial security turns out not to be trustworthy.

But when you create a trust, you document your wishes and expectations in a way that makes them enforceable instructions. When you formally transfer assets "in trust," you retain control of how your assets are used, when changes to the assets can be made, and who will receive those assets when the time is right.

WHAT IS A TRUST, ANYWAY?

At the most basic level, every trust is a contract. A trust is an agreement between two people, made for the benefit of a third person.

Sometimes we describe a trust as being like a triangle. Figure 2 on the next page shows how this triangle illustrates the relationships between the three parties to a trust.

At the top left corner of the triangle is the person who creates the trust. In our office, we call them the **grantor**, but they can also be called the settlor, the trustor, or the trustmaker.

The grantor makes all the decisions regarding the terms of the trust. To put it another way: the creator of the trust writes the rules that control the assets in the trust.

At the bottom-left corner of the triangle we find the person who manages the trust. This person is called the **trustee**.

When the trustee signs the trust document or an acceptance of trust, they agree to follow the terms of the trust document as written by the grantor.

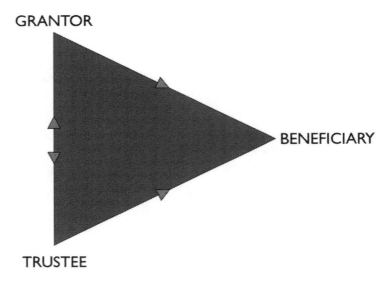

FIGURE 2

Finally, at the other side of the triangle, we find the **beneficiary**. The beneficiary is the person who receives the benefits of the trust.

On each leg of the triangle, I've drawn arrows to indicate how the relationship works. The leg between the grantor and the trustee has arrows pointing both directions to indicate that the trust document is a two-way street. The grantor and the trustee agree together about the management of the trust.

The other two legs of the triangle only have one arrow. This indicates that the trust agreement is a one-way street to the benefit of the beneficiary. In fact, even the triangle itself points from the grantor and the trustee toward the beneficiary.

The "trust triangle" is a simple diagram that applies to every trust, but it only defines the relationships and describes how the trust gets created. The actual operation of the trust is represented by a different diagram.

ONLY HALF THE BATTLE

Creating and signing your trust agreement is only half the battle when you want to use a trust in your estate plan. In order for your trust to function as intended, you also need to transfer assets into your trust. This process is commonly referred to as **trust funding**.

> The creator of the trust writes the rules that *control* the assets in the trust.

Without placing assets in the trust, the rules you just set in place in the agreement regarding your hopes, intentions, and goals, will have no effect.

You can think about your trust and the trust funding as if you have an empty bucket (the trust) and need to fill it up (the funding).

Figure 3 on the next page shows an example of what trust funding might look like.

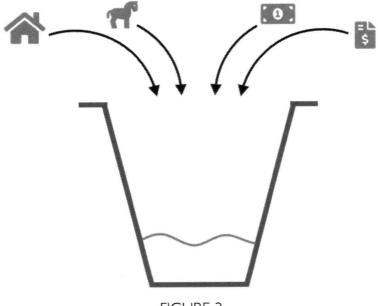

FIGURE 3

Because the trust allows you to appoint beneficiaries for all of the assets inside the bucket, it is usually a good idea to funnel as much of your net worth through the bucket as possible. You do that either by changing the ownership of your assets to the trust or by changing the beneficiaries on your accounts to list the trust.

When funding your trust, the types of assets you own will dictate how the ownership or beneficiary designations are listed for each of those assets. One simple example is the difference between your home, which is usually retitled to make the trust the owner, and your 401(k) which cannot be retitled in the trust and must instead have a beneficiary designation listed.

Another factor you need to consider when funding your trust is what conditions or protections your trust sets up, both for yourself and your kids. In some cases, it might be unwise to just give your kids your home or life savings at your death. If you include protections for them in the trust terms, you'll want to consider funneling your life insurance or retirement accounts into the trust, so those protections apply to all of the assets.

Obviously, every single person is different and has different goals for their assets. In fact, because you and your family are unique and have unique needs and desires that will almost certainly change over time, there's a better way to think about using your trust to allocate your home and life savings. We call it **asset alignment**.

Asset alignment involves getting each of your assets to point in the same direction as your trust. If the trust pulls the assets in, and the assets push in the direction the trust is pulling, your home and life savings can be aligned with your goals, making things easier and more efficient for you and your family in the end.

Then, as your goals change, you can easily adjust the trust document and the asset alignment to make sure everything is still working together.

IS YOUR TRUST HALF-EMPTY OR HALF-FULL?

Creating the trust agreement is where a lot of your time is spent. You need to make decisions about who should be the trustee, how the trustee will handle the assets, who gets what and when.

But just creating your trust doesn't do you any good. If you want the trust to protect your estate according to your goals, it is equally important to align all of your assets with the trust.

Speaking of protection, now that you know how trusts work, we'll look at some of the different types of trusts you can use in your estate planning in the next chapter.

"It does not do to leave a live dragon out of your calculations if you live near one."

J.R.R. Tolkien

CHAPTER 5

TRUSTS: WHAT'S IN A NAME?

There are probably as many different types of trusts as there are lawyers to draft them. In fact, choosing the right kind of trust for your specific situation and needs is a bit like getting the right medication for a medical condition. You need a doctor to get the right prescription, and you need a lawyer to get the right kind of trust.

As we take this 10,000-foot review of trusts, it's important to remember that every trust can be described by the "trust triangle" in Figure 2 on page 38.

WANTED: DEAD OR ALIVE

The first classification of trusts is based on timing. To figure out what kind of trust you are dealing with in this context, you have to answer the question, "When does the trust get created?"

When you read articles online or talk to a financial advisor about trusts, you're most likely to get advice about a **living trust**. A living trust is exactly what it sounds like: a trust you create while you are living. It might also be called an

inter vivos trust, which is just a Latin phrase that means "created during life."

The alternative to a living trust is a **testamentary trust**. Obviously, if you are the grantor of a trust, you have to be alive in order to define the terms of the trust agreement. So how do you differentiate between a living trust and a testamentary trust?

When I am reviewing whether a trust exists, I look for two or three key pieces of information. First, I want to know whether the trust has been signed by the grantor. Second, I look for documentation that the named trustee has accepted their role, usually by signing the trust itself or possibly with an acceptance of trust. Finally, I want to know if the trust has been funded. Have assets been placed into the bucket? (see Figure 3 on page 40)

The difference between a living trust and a testamentary trust is the timing of trustee control and trust funding. If a trustee doesn't get appointed for the trust until after your death, then the trust is probably testamentary. Likewise, if the trust doesn't get funded until after your death, then the trust is probably (though not always) testamentary.

Sometimes we look at the document that creates the trust relationship to see if a trust is inter vivos or testamentary. If your last will and testament sets up a trust to hold your kids' inheritance, that's a testamentary trust. If you sign a standalone trust agreement and transfer assets to the trustee under that agreement right away, that's a living trust.

REVOCABLE VS. IRREVOCABLE

The second important classification of a trust is whether it is revocable or irrevocable.

A trust is considered **revocable** if the grantor of the trust has the power to change the trust terms or cancel the trust at any time. Perhaps the most common type of trust is the *revocable living trust*.

In a revocable living trust, the grantor of the trust keeps total access to and can make all the management decisions for the assets in the trust. If you choose this type of trust, you can appoint yourself in all three corners of the trust triangle, making you the trustee and the beneficiary of the trust as well as the grantor.

Even if you don't put yourself in those roles, because you can change or cancel the trust at any time, you can override anything the trustee does or impose limits on the beneficiaries as you see fit.

If I were to draw you a picture of a traditional revocable living trust, I might draw a bucket with no lid (Figure 4). The bucket is open or unsealed because you can access and use the assets in the trust just like you could before you created the trust. For example, you, as the trustmaker, can buy and sell real estate or stocks held in the trust.

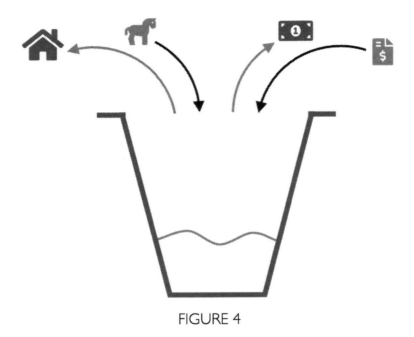

FIGURE 4

Because you are the creator of the trust, you use the trust document to set the rules for the trust. For example, the revocable living trust allows you to define when you should be considered to be disabled and who takes over control of the trust if you do become disabled or after your death.

A revocable living trust is a highly flexible, dynamic document. It allows you to maintain full use, control, and management of your assets. When you pass away, the trust's terms control how the trust's assets are allocated and distributed. The trust is a contract that controls this process, so your family can avoid probate which lets them set their own timing and keeps your financial affairs and their inheritance out of the public eye.

As an added bonus, because the trust stays out of probate, you have the flexibility to give more detailed instructions and create protections for your descendants. Those same protections would become difficult to implement and enforce if a court was supervising the administration of the trust.

EXAMPLE

I recently met with a widow in her 70s – we'll call her Linda. Linda's husband passed away a few years ago, and she wanted to visit with me about updating her estate plan.

Linda's husband was an active farmer right up until his death, working in partnership with their son on dozens of different opportunities. Even though he had a net worth of nearly $4,000,000, Linda's husband was so busy with actual farming that he never got around to setting up a business succession plan.

As a result, all of his business entities and real estate got tied up in probate for 18 months. That process cost Linda almost $85,000 in legal fees and costs. She was worried that costs like that would force a sale of the family farm and force her son into a bad financial position after her death.

I advised Linda that a revocable trust would keep the farm businesses out of probate, saving her kids thousands of dollars and keeping the family financial affairs out of the public eye.

Then we discussed how the trust would work, both during her life and after her death. Linda expressed concern that her daughter or, worse, the bank might force her son to sell out of some of the businesses or real estate.

To address this concern, we took two approaches. First, we specifically allocated several entities to Linda's son and offset that with rental homes that will go to her daughter. Second, and more importantly, because the revocable trust would keep them out of probate, we were able to design a testamentary subtrust to protect the farmland. Linda's son will be able to continue operating the family farm, and both of Linda's kids will have financial support from that farm as long as they live.

Generally speaking, an **irrevocable trust** is the opposite of a revocable trust: it's a trust where the <u>grantor</u> does not have the ability to change or cancel the trust agreement. In the end, every trust will become irrevocable if it lasts long enough.

For example, if you create a revocable living trust today, that trust will become irrevocable upon your death because you are no longer able to change its terms. Similarly, all testamentary trusts are also irrevocable trusts, since they get created because of the grantor's death.

Because you personally can't change the terms of an irrevocable trust, irrevocable trusts created during the grantor's life are designed for a specific purpose. Their names often look a bit like alphabet soup: MAPT or VAPT, QIT or MAIT, ILIT, IDGT, GRAT, and so on.

In my law practice, the most common irrevocable trust we create for our clients is used to protect their assets from the high costs of long-term care. There are several reasons an irrevocable trust is the best tool for that purpose.

When you create a *revocable* trust, you have the ability to take things out of the trust bucket whenever you want or need to. If you have total access to the assets inside the trust, state and federal law say that your creditors also have access to those assets. For all practical purposes, the trust assets are treated like they belong to you personally.

But in an *irrevocable* trust, once assets are placed in the trust bucket, the grantor of the trust can't take them back out again. They aren't available to you whenever you want, so they also aren't available to your creditors. That is, if you put your home and life savings in an irrevocable trust well before you need long-term care, then the nursing home won't be able to reach those assets when it comes time to pay for that care.

If I were to draw you a picture of this type of irrevocable trust, I might draw a bucket with the lid on and a handle so someone else can carry it, like the one in Figure 4. By sealing the top of the bucket and handing it to the trustee, the grantor can't just reach into the bucket whenever they want.

FIGURE 5

There are alternatives to using an irrevocable trust in this context. For example, we talked in Chapter Four about giving your assets to your kids now. Obviously, if your kids own your home, it won't be available to the nursing home.

Two problems with that approach, as we discussed in Chapter Four, are that it can create tax liability for your kids if the house is ever sold and you could lose your home if one of the kids gets into financial trouble or passes away.

> If your goal is to protect family assets,
> you should create an irrevocable trust
> as soon as possible.

The irrevocable trust acts like a holding tank between you and your children, allowing you to get the protection you need without risking loss of your home and life savings due to challenges in your children's lives.

And even though you can't take assets out of the trust bucket and put them in your own pocket, you can give the trustee of the trust the ability to distribute cash or property from the trust to your kids or grandkids.

If you want to implement a complete asset protection plan, keeping some assets available to you personally and protecting other assets, the best approach might be to set up both a revocable living trust and an irrevocable trust. You can place the funds that should be readily available for things like groceries, utilities, vacations, or anything else you wish into the revocable trust. The assets you want to protect would be placed into the irrevocable trust.

Timing is crucial when it comes to asset protection. For example, there is a five-year lookback period when you apply for Medicaid/Title 19 assistance with the nursing home bill. If you apply for that benefit sooner than five years after setting up the irrevocable trust, you will be penalized for trying to protect the assets you put in the trust.

Therefore, if your goal is to protect family assets, you should create an irrevocable trust as soon as possible.

EXAMPLE

I first met with Robert in the summer of 2016 after his wife, June, had received an early-onset Alzheimer's diagnosis. Robert was concerned about having to sell the farm he inherited from his mom to pay for June's care someday.

Robert and June had some money saved, and they had purchased a couple of chronic care insurance policies, so Robert was feeling pretty good about being able to take care of June and keep working in his handyman business at the same time.

June's diagnosis was quite recent at that time, so Robert decided to create an irrevocable trust to protect the farm. He figured, between the insurance and their savings, it would be at least five years before June would need more help than he could provide on his own.

After a couple of years, June's Alzheimer's started getting progressively worse. She quickly reached a point where Robert had to tap into their chronic care insurance. By the beginning of 2021, June needed 24/7 care. Robert couldn't quit his job, and the insurance benefits only had a few months left.

But because Robert had created an irrevocable trust far enough ahead of time, by the end of 2021, we were able to apply for Medicaid benefits for June's nursing home bill. The state ignored Robert's farm because he had moved it out of his name more than five years before.

A FEW LOOSE ENDS

In the last two chapters, we've spent some time focused on how to avoid the government's plan, stay out of probate, and protect your assets from creditors, both during your life and after your death, using trusts.

We've also talked about how trusts help you allocate your assets the way you want, when you want, and to the people you want. Check out the table on the next page for a comparison of the different types of trusts.

But even with all of those benefits, trusts can't do it all.

Don't get me wrong – trusts are a vitally important tool for accomplishing your goals. By creating detailed and specific instructions for your trustee or personal representative, you ensure your family knows and follows your intent for your financial resources.

But what if someone needs to step in and make decisions for you, in your place? Medical decisions often need to be made in the moment, based on all the facts and circumstances. Who will do that if you are in a coma? Who signs papers on your behalf if you need a nursing home, and who has access to your retirement accounts to keep your bills paid?

Your trust can't appoint someone to act as your substitute decisionmaker, and that's arguably the most important role in your plan. We'll look at how you can appoint those decisionmakers in the next chapter.

	Will	Revocable Living Trust	Irrevocable Living Trust
Provide for Distribution of Assets After Death	✓	✓	✓
Avoid Government's Probate Process	✗	✓	✓
Allows You to Select Who Manages Your Assets if You Become Disabled	✗	✓	✓
Provides Lifetime Asset Protection from Creditors and Nursing Home	✗	✗	✓
Protects Assets from Estate Recovery after Death	✗	✗	✓

"The time to repair the roof is when the sun is shining."

John F. Kennedy

CHAPTER 6

THE MOST IMPORTANT ESTATE PLANNING TOOL?

It's "common knowledge" that you need to get your will done. Your financial adviser, your CPA, and even your doctor will all tell you to get your will in place. And that's good advice.

But what you're about to read may surprise you.

Your will is not the most important part of your estate plan.

We've already spent a fair amount of time talking about what a will does: arrange your affairs once you have passed away. Your will gives you a way to leave instructions about who inherits your stuff, who is in charge of distributing your stuff, and (if you have young kids) who takes care of your kids.

But we've also talked quite a bit about what your will <u>does not</u> do for you: avoid probate, protect assets (for both you and your kids), and arrange things for when you become incapacitated.

A trust is more effective than a will at directing your financial affairs. And since it's a contract that starts to benefit you as soon as you align your assets with it, a trust provides some protection right away by giving the trustee mandatory instructions for taking care of your money and property.

But the trustee's authority is limited to the assets you transferred into the trust. They don't have authority over anything outside the trust (things like IRAs or life insurance policies), and they don't have the ability to step in as substitute decisionmaker when you lose the ability to make decisions on your own.

Since your will doesn't start working until after your death, and a trust is a contract governing only the management of assets inside the trust bucket, you need one more tool to make sure someone can step in and make decisions on your behalf: the power of attorney.

> Your will is not the most important
> part of your estate plan.

A **power of attorney** allows you to designate a person you want to have act on your behalf or in your place. The person you name in a power of attorney is called the **agent** because their decisions have the same authority and effect as decisions you would make.

Most people – and many lawyers – treat the power of attorney as a minor document and the choice of agent as less important within your estate planning. But the agent under a power of attorney has a lot of responsibility and authority.

After all, that person has the same access to and control over your personal assets and medical information as you have!

There are two main categories of power of attorney involved in a well-designed estate plan: financial and medical. A **financial power of attorney** is also called a **general power of attorney** because the agent is granted broad authority over all of the common financial matters you might deal with yourself on a day-to-day basis.

With your agent having so much access and control over your finances, it's important to be careful about who, when, and how your power of attorney takes on their role and when their authority ends. Let's talk about those things next.

IT MIGHT AS WELL BE SPRING-ING

You have two basic options for when your financial power of attorney becomes effective: **immediate** or **springing**.

In an *immediate* power of attorney, the agent you appoint takes on their role right away. You give them all the powers of the power of attorney relationship before your signature is even dry.

If you're like me, you probably don't want your family members to have access to and control over your assets until it's absolutely necessary. In that situation, we would use a *springing* power of attorney. When a power of attorney is considered to be "springing" you define a certain condition or conditions that must be met before your agent is granted access and control over your finances. Typically, this condition requires a formal determination that you are incapacitated (like we talked about in the Introduction).

At Huizenga Law, we prepare *mostly* springing powers of attorney, but there are situations where an immediate power of attorney is the better choice. In addition, our springing power of attorney includes the option of using a signed authorization to "release the spring" early, before incapacity occurs.

MADE TO LAST

We've talked about how a power of attorney creates an agency relationship with the person you appoint. In an agency relationship, you are the principal, and the person you appoint is your agent. As a result, it's a little like that person is your clone, able to do anything you can do.

But if that's the case, then when you become incapacitated and are unable to manage your own financial affairs, the agent and the agency relationship would also be unable to act on your behalf.

If you're thinking, "I thought the power of attorney was supposed to avoid that problem," you are 100% correct. If the power of attorney ended because you became incapacitated, then no one would ever sign a power of attorney!

To address this problem, it's vital that your general/financial power of attorney be designated as **durable**.

By signing a durable springing financial power of attorney, you can name the person who should step in and manage your financial affairs even and especially when you are no longer able to do so without giving them the power to sign documents or move money in your name right away.

INFORMED CONSENT AND THE HEALTHCARE AGENT

A financial power of attorney document doesn't give your agent authority over medical decisions. For that, you use a **healthcare power of attorney**. Other names for this document include **medical power of attorney** or **medical proxy**.

When you appoint an agent under a medical power of attorney, that document is almost always effective immediately because your doctor will always defer to your ability to give informed consent.

If you think back to the Introduction to this book, you'll recall that your medical decision-making has two parts: you have to be able to understand and you have to be able to communicate. If you possess both of these elements, the doctor will only ever ask you about decisions regarding your medical care.

It's when you either no longer understand or have lost *all* ability to communicate your wishes (or both) that the doctor turns to your healthcare agent.

The many forms of dementia are common ailments that cause you to lose your ability to understand a medical decision. Examples where you can't communicate your wishes might include being under anesthesia during surgery or being unconscious following an accident.

There is one common situation where having a medical power of attorney might not sufficiently protect your wishes: the persistent vegetative state.

I DON'T WANT TO BE A VEGETABLE

Maybe you've heard someone say that. Maybe you've said it yourself. After all, while the statement "I don't want to be a vegetable" is maybe a little … rough around the edges … the goal is quite common. It's the sentiment that means, "If I have no brain activity, I don't want to be kept alive by machines."

If you find yourself worrying about what will happen to you if you enter a persistent vegetative state, there's a tool you can use to address those concerns: a **living will**.

While a health care power of attorney appoints someone to make medical decisions on your behalf at the moment a decision is needed, in a living will, you take on the decision-making yourself ahead of time. A living will is the set of instructions you want your family and your doctor to follow if you are so physically frail or nonresponsive that the only reason you are still alive is because you have machines performing all your essential bodily functions.

Because the living will contains your directions for your medical care, it is often referred to as an **advance healthcare directive**.

Signing a living will is entirely your choice. There may be a wide variety of personal – philosophical, spiritual, moral – reasons for you personally not to sign one. But the living will can play an important role within our definition of estate planning. It's another way to provide for yourself or your loved ones if you become incapacitated.

With a signed living will, you take the choice of "pulling the plug" off your family's shoulders. If you choose not to sign a living will, then the decisions about your end-of-life care remain the responsibility of your agent under your health care power of attorney. Both are completely valid approaches – make sure you do what is right for you!

Sometimes I get asked about adding a "DNR" to my clients' medical directives. Strictly speaking, a "DNR" – **do not resuscitate** – order is unique to a particular admission into a medical facility.

For example, it is common for residents of nursing homes to sign a DNR upon admission into the nursing facility, and often that DNR stays in effect until they pass away. But a person going in for major surgery might sign a DNR when

HIPAA PERMITS DISCLOSURE OF IPOST TO OTHER HEALTH CARE PROVIDERS AS NECESSARY		
Iowa Physician Orders for Scope of Treatment (IPOST) First follow these orders, **THEN** contact the physician, nurse practitioner or physician's assistant. This is a medical order sheet based on the person's current medical condition and treatment preferences. Any section not completed implies full treatment for that section. Everyone shall be treated with dignity and respect.		**Last Name** **First/Middle Name** **Date of Birth**

A Check one	**CARDIOPULMONARY RESUSCITATION (CPR):** Person has no pulse **AND** is not breathing. ☐ CPR/Attempt Resuscitation ☐ DNR/Do Not Attempt Resuscitation
B Check one	**MEDICAL INTERVENTIONS:** Person has a pulse **AND/OR** is breathing. ☐ **COMFORT MEASURES ONLY** Use medication by any route, positioning, wound care and other measures to relieve pain and suffering. Use oxygen, suction and manual treatment of airway obstruction as needed for comfort. *Patient prefers no transfer to hospital for life-sustaining treatment. Transfer if comfort needs cannot be met in current location.* ☐ **LIMITED ADDITIONAL INTERVENTIONS** Includes care described above. Use medical treatment, cardiac monitor, oral/IV fluids and medications as indicated. **Do not use intubation,** or mechanical ventilation. May consider less invasive airway support (BiPAP, CPAP). May use vasopressors. *Transfer to hospital if indicated, may include critical care.* ☐ **FULL TREATMENT** Includes care described above. Use intubation, advanced airway interventions, mechanical ventilation and cardioversion as indicated. *Transfer to hospital if indicated. Includes critical care.* Additional Orders: _____
C Check one	**ARTIFICIALLY ADMINISTERED NUTRITION** Always offer food by mouth if feasible. ☐ No artificial nutrition by tube. ☐ Defined trial period of artificial nutrition by tube. ☐ Long-term artificial nutrition by tube.

D	**MEDICAL DECISION MAKING**	
	Directed by: (listed in order of Iowa Code/Statute for Priority of Surrogates; check only one) ☐ Patient ☐ Durable Power of Attorney for Health Care ☐ Spouse ☐ Majority of Adult Children ☐ Parents ☐ Majority rule for nearest relative ☐ Other: _____	**Rationale for these orders:** (check all that apply) ☐ Advance Directives ☐ Patient's known preference ☐ Limited treatment options ☐ Poor prognosis ☐ Other: _____

Physician/ARNP/PA signature (mandatory)	Print Physician/ARNP/PA Name	Date	Phone Number
Patient/Resident or Legal Surrogate for Health Care Signature as identified above (mandatory)		Date	

SEND IPOST WITH PERSON WHENEVER TRANSFERRED OR DISCHARGED

DOCUMENT THAT IPOST FORM WAS TRANSFERRED WITH PERSON

This is a sample IPOST. Visit www.itsnottoolatebooks.com/resources for a link to the state's most current free version.

FIGURE 7

they are admitted for the surgery, but that DNR would end when they are later discharged from the hospital.

Another end-of-life care option for residents of Iowa is the Iowa Physician Order for Scope of Treatment, or **IPOST**. With an IPOST designation, the wishes you express in your living will become a doctor's order in your medical chart. As a result, an IPOST must be signed by your physician. A sample of the 2022 IPOST form is provided in Figure 7 on the previous page.

The DNR and the IPOST are relatively recent concepts in end-of-life care planning, and they are both optional and extremely individualized. Not everyone will want or need one.

But the power of attorney documents – general/financial and healthcare/medical – are _absolutely essential_ parts of your estate plan. So much so, that I would call the power of attorney the most important estate planning document.

DON'T BELIEVE ME?

If you're not convinced that the financial and medical power of attorney documents are the most important tools in the estate planning toolbox, let me tell you a story.

> **EXAMPLE**
>
> Richard was a single man – divorced, actually – in his late 70s. Richard never had kids. His ex-wife died in 2003. His closest living relative was a cousin in New Mexico, so Richard came to rely heavily on his neighbors, the Jacksons.

The Jacksons knew Richard was showing signs of dementia, so they kept a close eye on him. One of Richard's habits involved walking his dog every morning at 8:00 and every afternoon at 4:00. Twice every day, Richard and his little, white ball of fur would slowly walk to a park 4 blocks from home, stroll around the block, and walk slowly back.

One Saturday afternoon in June, Mr. Jackson was outside mowing his lawn when he realized he hadn't seen Richard that day. He rang Richard's front doorbell and knocked loudly, but no one answered. As he made his way around to the back door, he could see Richard through the window.

Richard had fallen sometime during the evening and had laid on his floor for hours. Mr. Jackson immediately called an ambulance and Richard was whisked away to the hospital.

After Richard was put in the ambulance, it was months before Mr. Jackson heard from him again. Due to a COVID-19 outbreak, he couldn't visit Richard in the hospital, and when Richard was discharged to a nursing home a couple weeks later, the hospital staff wouldn't tell Mr. Jackson where Richard had moved to.

In the meantime, Richard was making small improvements thanks to the nursing home staff's diligent care. But it wasn't long before the nursing home bill came due. With no family around to make decisions on Richard's behalf, one of the nursing home employees (the social worker) filed a petition to be appointed Richard's guardian and conservator. Three months, a background check, two court hearings, and $4,000 later, a judge finally appointed her to handle Richard's affairs.

As conservator, the social worker then spent several months trying to decipher Richard's finances. It turned out that he was renting his home and was behind on rent by six months. After reviewing his checking account and calling each of the companies taking automatic payments out each month, the social worker discovered that Richard had two life insurance policies as well.

After a year of work and searching, the nursing home social worker had moved all of Richard's belongings out of his residence, cashed out his life insurance, and found a new home for his dog with the Jacksons.

(The Jacksons were relieved to finally get an update on Richard's circumstances – he'd had a small stroke, but was fully recovered – and were happy to take her in.)

But the nursing home bill was now over $70,000 and climbing each month. And the head nurse kept pushing the social worker to sign a Do Not Resuscitate (DNR) directive for Richard. In the end, the social worker left her position due to the stress of balancing Richard's needs with her job responsibilities.

Another year passed and, in an effort to satisfy the nursing home, the (former) social worker asked the Court to approve her signing of a DNR on Richard's behalf as his guardian. Since the social worker was not related to

Richard, the judge appointed a separate lawyer to make sure Richard's best interests were being protected and scheduled a hearing to determine whether a DNR was appropriate in Richard's situation.

Imagine being the Jacksons and having a neighbor you care about just vanish without a trace.

Imagine being the social worker whose employer demanded you do whatever it takes to get a resident's bill paid – even if that means going to court. Worse, imagine having to balance your job's demands with your duty to look out for that resident's best interests.

But the nursing home wasn't in the wrong, either. Their books were $70,000 behind, and something had to give.

Imagine being in Richard's place and having someone you don't know making Do Not Resuscitate decisions for you!

IT'S NOT TOO LATE TO GET STARTED

If Richard had appointed Mr. or Mrs. Jackson or even his cousin in New Mexico as financial and medical power of attorney ahead of time, things would have gone much more smoothly for Richard and for the people around him.

He would have had a decisionmaker when he lost the ability to make his own decisions. His bills would have been paid or cancelled on time, likely saving him thousands of dollars.

But most importantly, if he'd gotten a power of attorney in place ahead of time, Richard's loved ones would have had peace of mind that he was in the best possible situation for his needs. But like a lot of people, Richard didn't know where to start, so he didn't start at all.

Just by reading this book, you're one step further along than Richard was. You know what tools are available to help you stay in control while you're alive and well. In this chapter, you've learned about the most important estate planning documents which will make sure you and your loved ones have what they need if you become incapacitated.

And you've learned how to give what you have to the people you want, when you want, in the way you want by avoiding the four main threats to your home and life savings: the government's plan, long-term care costs, creditors, and predators.

Most importantly: *you know you need to get your planning done while you still have the capacity to make your own decisions.*

But there's one thing we haven't talked much about: why it all matters. That's because the "why" is up to you. Let's revisit your legacy in the next chapter.

"If you don't know where you are going,
you'll end up someplace else."

Yogi Berra

CHAPTER 7

THE ESTATE PLANNING JOURNEY

We've spent a lot of time in this book talking about the tools and strategies involved in estate planning. We've looked at the government's plan for your care and your finances. We've looked at how wills work after you die and how trusts work during your life. And we've looked at powers of attorney both for financial and medical decision-making.

Proper estate planning leverages all these different tools to do three things:

1. Keep you in control as long as you are alive and well,
2. Take care of yourself and your loved ones if you become incapacitated or disabled, and
3. Give what you have to the people you want, when you want, and in the way you want.

Now's as good a time as any to take notice of something very important about our definition of estate planning: it's focused on *you* and *what you want*.

That doesn't mean estate planning is self-centered. What it means is: proper, effective estate planning is about accomplishing *your goals* so you can leave *your legacy*.

MOTIVATED BY FEAR

When I talk about proper estate planning, I'm referring to the *process* a person follows to get their wishes down on paper. The most common "approach" has three steps:

1. Fear
2. Find
3. Forget

Most people start thinking about their estate planning for at least one of four main reasons. We've talked about versions of them throughout this book:

- You're afraid you will lose your home and life savings to the high cost of nursing home care.
- You're afraid your untrustworthy son- or daughter-in-law will burn through the inheritance you leave for your kids.
- You're afraid no one will be able (or willing) to step in and take care of your home and life savings if you become incapacitated.
- You're afraid your home and life savings will be reduced or consumed by the complications and expenses of probate.

Motivated by these fears, they do a little Googling to come up with a "lawyer near me" and pay them a visit. The lawyer asks who they want to give their money to and who should be executor. They might ask how much money the person has just in case they "have enough to need a trust."

The lawyer has their staff fill in the blanks on a word processing template, the person signs everything a couple weeks later, and they put it in a drawer, never to be seen again, all the while congratulating themselves for "getting a will."

Or maybe they head to an office supply store or a big-box store and buy an "estate planning workbook." They fill in the blanks themselves, sign it, and get it notarized. Maybe they do a little extra research and find a "state form" for a power of attorney where they can also fill in the blanks themselves.

But you're smarter than that. This far into the book, you've figured out why both these solutions won't get the job done. In the first example, the person only got a will prepared because that's all they asked for. They "didn't have enough" to need a trust and didn't sign a power of attorney, so there's no lifetime protection. At all.

In the second example, they didn't have their will signed properly – it needs two witnesses, not a notary – so not only is there no trust, but the will won't do anything for them either because it's not valid.

Not to mention the fact that the documents aren't personal at all. Filling in blanks on a standard form simply doesn't cut it when it comes to your personal legacy.

THE LEGACYGUARD™ PROCESS – A BETTER WAY

In this book, I've talked about the four threats to your home and life savings. And those threats are all present in the fears I described above: nursing home costs, creditors and predators, incapacity, and probate. But there's no reason to be *afraid* of these things.

Because you've got the tools you need to avoid them.

Now, all you need is help figuring out how to apply those tools in the most effective and efficient way. In my law firm, our trademark LegacyGuard Process applies to all the planning we do. It starts with three steps or phases:

1. Vision
2. Design
3. Sign and Align

We begin the LegacyGuard Process with Vision to help you find clarity and focus on what's most important to you. A Vision Meeting with my law firm is designed to cut through the fears that might be clouding your vision for your legacy.

After your Vision Meeting, you'll leave our office with a positive outlook. We'll help you see that it's possible to avoid the threats to your legacy and accomplish the goals you have for your care, your home and life savings, and your loved ones.

Your Vision Meeting gives me and my team a clear picture of what your highest and best hopes are for you   r legacy. With that picture clearly defined, we can develop a plan to make that picture a reality. That's the first step in the Design phase. We call it "building your CASL."

"CASL" stands for **Comprehensive Analysis and Strategy Letter**, and we build it for you in two parts: a written description of how your plan will work and a visual presentation of the available strategies to accomplish your goals.

Once your CASL is ready, it's time for your Design Meeting. The written description is the letter that we mail you before your Design Meeting, and the presentation helps guide the conversation during that meeting. Once you've settled on the right approach, we'll revisit your goals with a series of questions that will help you make the specific decisions that will accomplish your specific desires.

Finally, with a clear Vision and a plan Designed to make that Vision a reality, our team can get to work building the legal machinery that will make your plan a reality. This last phase is where the rubber meets the road. You came looking for – and found – answers. Now it's time for us to put those answers to use.

If the tools involved in your plan include a revocable or irrevocable trust, we won't just write up the legal documents. We'll also prepare the letters, deeds, and other documentation needed to align your assets with your trust. After all, what good is your trust if it isn't funded?

You sign all your documents and set your plan in motion at the Sign and Align Meeting. Then, after the Sign and Align meeting, our Asset Alignment process includes filing deeds to transfer property into your trust and communicating with your financial advisers and banks to make sure your needed changes are completed on time. But then we go one step further with phase four and our one-of-a-kind LegacyGuard Program.

Guarding your legacy starts with a Family Care Meeting where you invite your loved ones, your advisors, or both to a meeting to review the goals you have and the choices you made to accomplish those goals.

But more than that, we created our LegacyGuard Program so that we could be there for you and your family when you need us most. In firms with a program like ours, you have continuous phone and email access to the entire planning team, including your lawyer; no-cost meetings with your lawyer when your goals or circumstances change; AAA (Asset Alignment Audit) service; and an annual plan review.

And that's just in your first year in the program.

You see, your estate plan is like a well-oiled, finely tuned machine. Over time, as you put the different tools to work, your estate plan will need maintenance. Your family will need to be trained on the latest upgrades. It's even possible the machine will need repairs.

With a program like the LegacyGuard Program at Huizenga Law, you have a team of experts performing regular maintenance on that high-performance machine, giving you peace of mind that your plan will continue to protect your home and life savings from the threats of nursing home costs, probate, incapacity, and predators and creditors.

I created the LegacyGuard Program because accomplishing your goals isn't a one-and-done thing. Sometimes life happens. It happens to you; it happens to your loved ones. If your circumstances, your priorities, or even your goals change, your LegacyGuard Program membership is there to help your plan pivot quickly to keep everything on track.

It's completely normal to start the estate planning process in response to worry or anxiety that someone or something is going to take your home and life savings away from you and your loved ones. But you don't have to stay in that fearful mindset.

With proper estate planning, you can take the reins and create a plan centered on you and your family. You can protect your home and life savings and leave a meaningful legacy for the people who matter most. It's not too late to get started.

> "Someone's sitting in the shade
> today because someone planted a tree
> a long time ago."
>
> Warren Buffett

CHAPTER 8

THE NEXT STEP

If you've made it to this chapter after reading this entire book, congratulations! More importantly, thank you for sharing some of your valuable time with me. I sincerely hope you were able to learn how your options for protecting your home and life savings are only limited by the legacy you want to leave when you're gone.

Every person has a different vision of what their financial future could and should look like. If estate planning means maintaining control of your finances while you're alive and well and taking care of yourself and your loved ones if you become incapacitated, then your vision should define what that planning looks like.

But estate planning is also about giving what you have to the people you love, when and how you think is best. Since every family has unique concerns driven by their distinct family makeup, your estate plan should reflect that makeup and address those concerns.

If your planning is driven by fear and assumptions about what is possible, it can do irreparable harm to your legacy. You deserve an advisor who can walk with you as you explore what's possible for your family while protecting that legacy. My team and I would be honored to help guide you to the solution that works on your timing, so you're not in this alone.

We have a saying around the office that goes something like this: The best time to do your estate planning was five years ago.

The second-best time is right now.

Contact my office to take the first step on that journey together with an in-person **Vision Meeting**. This no-obligation appointment will last about an hour, and our experienced team will help you find clarity around your individual situation and needs. At the end of the meeting you can decide if you want to continue down the path with us as your guide.

To schedule a meeting with our office:

- Call us at 712-737-3885
- Visit www.huizengalaw.com/book-a-call

Thank you again for reading this book. Please reach out to me, so I can help whenever you need it.

The best time to do your estate planning was five years ago. The second-best time is right now.

RESOURCES

At times throughout *It's Not Too Late: How to Protect Your Home, and Life Savings in Iowa*, I have referenced a number of additional resources which are available for readers of this book and clients of the Huizenga Law Firm.

Rather than republish the book every year to update these references, we have created a reader-only webpage that we keep updated with new resources and as the law changes.

To access this private page, please visit:

www.itsnottoolatebooks.com/resources

ABOUT THE AUTHOR

Author and attorney Ethan Huizenga has focused exclusively on Medicaid eligibility planning and estate planning (including trusts, estates, wills, powers of attorney, and gifting issues) since graduating from Saint Louis University School of Law in 2008.

Ethan is licensed to practice law in Iowa, South Dakota, and Missouri. He cut his teeth in Elder Law in the St. Louis metro area after law school, and now owns and runs The Huizenga Law Firm, P.C., in Orange City, Iowa, where he has helped hundreds of people protect their home, family farm, and life savings from the threats posed by probate, creditors and predators, nursing home expenses, and unexpected incapacity.

Ethan is a member of WealthCounsel, ElderCounsel, and the National Academy of Elder Law Attorneys (NAELA), as well as the Elder Law Section, the Trust & Estate Planning Section, and the Probate Section of the Iowa Bar.

Ethan has presented for a variety of non-profit organizations, businesses, lawyer groups, and consumers on topics including Estate Planning, Medicaid Planning, Probate, Trust Administration, and Aging in Place.

In 2019, Ethan launched his revolutionary LegacyGuard Program to provide ongoing support to individuals and families concerned about losing their financial and personal legacies due to sudden illness and incapacity, dementia, long-term care expenses, creditors, and death costs.

To learn more about Ethan, The Huizenga Law Firm, and the LegacyGuard Program visit www.huizengalaw.com.

A SMALL REQUEST

First, let me say one more sincere thank you for reading *It's Not Too Late: How to Protect Your Home and Life Savings in Iowa*. I trust you found answers to your questions in these pages and that you have a clear roadmap for how you can protect everyone and everything that's important to you.

I do have one small favor to ask: would you mind taking a few moments to leave an honest review for this book on Amazon? Reviews are the BEST way to help people just like you find this book and get the answers they need. Plus, I check all my reviews looking for helpful feedback. Visit:

www.itsnottoolatebooks.com/review-ep

If you have additional questions or would like to schedule a Vision Meeting to discuss how our LegacyGuard process can help you protect your home and life savings, schedule an initial call here: www.planforthenursinghome.com/book-a-call. We'd love to hear from you!

DON'T FORGET THIS!

IS YOUR
ESTATE PLAN
READY?

As an exclusive and special gift for readers of *It's Not Too Late: How to Protect Your Home and Life Savings in Iowa*, my team and I have created this essential checklist that you can use to assess whether your estate plan will accomplish your wishes.

By answering the questions in *Is Your Estate Plan Ready?* you'll discover whether your will or trust is adequate for your needs and where you might need to shore things up.

Think your will is good enough for you?
Take this **EXCLUSIVE ASSESSMENT**
and find out for sure!

SPECIAL BONUS GIFT

www.ItsNotTooLateBooks.com/assessment

Made in the USA
Middletown, DE
25 August 2024

59093859R00075